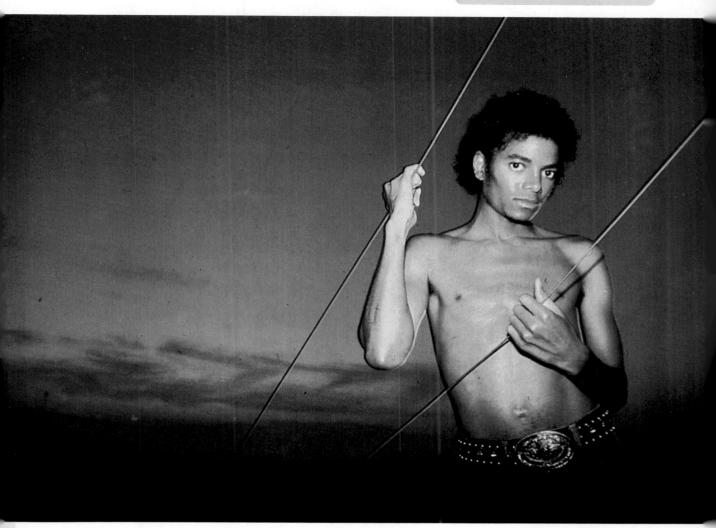

Michael Jackson

Introduction by Robin Katz

Introduction

THE FIRST TIME I MET MICHAEL JACKSON, indeed all of the Jackson brothers and their father Joseph, was on 29 October 1972. Michael was 14 years old. The date sticks in my mind because it was Randy Jackson's tenth birthday. The family was arriving in London for its first British tour. At 6.30 am, they were due in on Pam Am flight 106.

First British tour

As an American then visiting London, I had volunteered to start a British fan club for The Jackson Five. Throughout the summer I worked on the floor outside Motown Records' tiny London office, trying to make myself so useful they would have to offer me work. Finally, I was declared a fire risk and was given a desk! Wearing two hats, my time was divided between my unpaid work at Motown and being a music journalist.

I launched a "Jackson Five" page in the weekly music newspaper *Record Mirror*. American Jackson Five fans had lots of magazines devoted solely to the group. My page was the only regular place where British Jackson Five fans could swap addresses, write love poems and have their questions answered.

With news of The Jackson Five's British concert dates, Motown asked me to join the group for their British tour. The "Jackson Five" page had also had official blessing to print the airport arrival time. Busloads of fan club members were organized to arrive at dawn. Only the security people at the airport had underestimated the group's fantastic popularity.

Badly shaken

That first glimpse of Michael Jackson was unforgettable. When the bleary-eyed Jacksons emerged from the customs area, the fans became so hysterical that they bolted towards the unprotected group. Chunky tour promoter Danny O'Donovan was trampled to the ground trying to protect Michael. He failed. In a frightening display of "love" one girl succeeded in yanking off Michael's shoe and two others tried to do the same with his hair. I can still hear his scream. Eventually, the police rushed the family to safety, but everyone involved was badly shaken.

The group never mentioned the incident again, perhaps regarding it as just part of the job. Their concert tour, like so many before and since, kicked off in great spirit. Fans were elated and cynics were converted. At 14, the 'm' in Michael could have stood for mischief. Certainly no reporter could better the questions he fired at *them*. "Where did you get that coat? ... Does it come in my size? ... Look at those red fingernails, are they real? ... Do you know any of the Beatles? Why not? Isn't this England?"

Some determined fans actually managed to meet the group only to find themselves suddenly completely lost for words. On such occasions, you could see Michael overcoming his own shyness to put them at their ease.

This book was devised and produced by
Multimedia Publications (UK) Ltd.

Editor Richard Horwich
Production Arnon Orbach
Design John Strange
Picture Research Paul Snelgrove

First published in Great Britain 1984 by
Books and Toys Ltd, The Grange,
Grange Yard, London SE1 3AG

ISBN 0 9509620 0 7

Colour origination by D.S. Colour International
Ltd, London. Printed in Spain by Cayfosa,
Barcelona. Dep. Leg. B. 14308/84

"Bubblegum idols"

In the mid-70s, the Jacksons returned to Britain to perform at the Royal Variety Show in Glasgow, Scotland, in front of the Queen. Again, they were a fantastic success. By this time, the hysteria that had accompanied the "bubblegum idols" on their last tour had died down sufficiently to enable the group to shop in London with only minor interruptions from fans. However, a friend and I still decided it would be safer if we smuggled Michael out of the hotel to see Big Ben.

We drove him round Trafalgar Square, Buckingham Palace, St. James's Park, down the embankment, past the Houses of Parliament, then Big Ben and on to the Tower of London. Michael returned the favor by helping us crash a post-concert party for star George Benson.

The last time I saw Michael he was beginning to gain a reputation in the press for being withdrawn. We drove together from London to Brighton. It was supposed to be an interview, but it turned into a pretty serious conversation. Michael had lost neither the curiosity nor the awareness he had always displayed.

Inspiration

We talked about growing. I told him about a songwriter named Gerry Goffin, whose songs were the backbone of my record collection. Recently, they had helped me through a grim patch. I was just becoming old enough to understand the feelings that Goffin had been writing about years earlier. Becoming a little too emotional, I turned away from Michael to compose myself. Within a split second, I felt a comforting hand on my shoulder. When I looked back at Michael, he was nodding his head and smiling. "I know how you feel", he said warmly. Then, he pointed to himself, to his heart. "Stevie Wonder", he whispered, making it clear who inspired him the way Goffin inspired me.

I was left with the feeling that Michael hadn't changed. He had emerged. He had stopped trying to be what other people wanted him to be. He wasn't ashamed to admit that he likes what others would call "corny" music as much as funky music. And he wasn't afraid to admit that he was vulnerable. He talked freely about how much he loved to let his imagination unravel.

Where Michael's imagination will take him next is anyone's guess. But one thing is certain – whatever he does will be successful. It could hardly be otherwise, for what follows is one of the greatest success stories of our time.

Robin Katz
London 1984

Chapter 1
The Jackson Five

The place is Gary, Indiana, an industrial city in the middle of America. The time is just over twenty years ago. The family is called Jackson. Father Joe is a crane driver and mother Katherine works part time at a department store. There are nine children, six boys and three girls.

Joe was once a guitarist, but his priorities have had to change to feed his family. So, he has put away his prized guitar – only to find his sons Tito and Jermaine playing it behind his back. At first he punishes them, then realizes they love music. So he rounds up his sons and turns them into a group.

After school, while other kids play sports, the Jackson kids rehearse. Their mother makes their costumes. At the weekend they pile into an old car, drive for hours to play concerts, sleep in the car and head back to school for Monday morning. They start to earn a reputation as a good, live act.

In the summer of 1968 The Jackson Five are allowed to perform in their home town of Gary. Diana Ross is there and quick to spot their talent. Suddenly, the local boys are going for the big time. They sign with Motown Records and soon after leave Gary to begin their new life on the pop circuit in Los Angeles.

I Want You Back

In 1969, The Jackson Five burst onto the music scene with their first hit, *I Want You Back*. Michael's appeal doubled with solo hits like *Got To Be There* and *Ben*, his favorite song from the early period. Peering from hundreds of magazine covers and blaring from thousands of radio speakers, The Jackson Five had become the uncrowned kings of pop.

Top right: Michael had a genuine flair for singing ballads even at the early age of 12. *Ben* was a song about a rat. When singing it in concert, the sense of drama was heightened by concentrating one spotlight on Michael while the rest of the stage was kept in total darkness.

Right: The Jackson Five during one of their early television appearances. In those days, Michael, Marlon and Jackie danced together while Tito and Jermaine played guitar.

Previous pages: Wanna be startin' somethin'? Young Michael gets a hand in front of brothers Marlon, Tito, Jackie and Jermaine (*left to right*).

Below: Michael at the height of his popularity as a "bubblegum idol" At the time of this photo, his smile alone was enough to cause hysteria.

Top right: Here's Michael in his hotel room preparing to go out and meet the press. The Jackson Five had a staff member to look after their stage clothing, but each brother was responsible for taking care of his casual clothes.

Right: One, two three, it's easy as ABC. Michael encourages the audience to join in on handclaps as The Jackson Five perform one of their early hits. To excite crowds further, Michael loved dancing from one end of the stage to another with dazzling speed.

Left: British Jackson Five fan club members wore special red and yellow badges. When the group arrived in Britain, Michael sported one too.

Below: What's Michael going to do next? Nobody knows for sure, but his brothers are keeping a watchful eye on him.

"What do you mean our mom dresses us funny?" Early on, Mrs Jackson made all the group's costumes, but by the time The Jackson Five were famous they wore specially designed outfits like these. In 1972, every fashion-conscious kid wanted to copy this style – pointed collars, flared trousers and platform boots.

Left: Meet the Jackson Six. In 1972, 10 year-old Randy Jackson joined his famous five brothers onstage and on record. Here *(top left)* Randy is photographed with the rest of the boys in London.

Above: A rare opportunity to see The Jacksons looking pretty ship-shape, dressed identically for an American television show. As lead singer, Michael is entitled to wear this flashier costume. The other brothers certainly seem happy enough just looking on.

The Jacksons knew how to celebrate in style – here they are dressed up formally for a glamorous evening out *(top left)*. And when the group made stage appearances they always looked really snappy *(bottom left)*. However, when

The Jackson Five accepted gold discs they showed a marked preference for the casual look *(top right)*. Michael *(bottom right)* clearly enjoys the elegant look as well, seen here with his father Joe.

Far left: Marlon, Jackie and Michael are the Jackson *Dancing Machine*. Jackie's the mastermind behind most of their dancing routines, including the one you see here.

Top: Marlon, Jackie and Michael look as though they're running a race. Actually, this is a live performance of *I Want You Back*.

Left: Michael demonstrating all the skills of a lead singer.

Chapter 2
Home – "fortress" Encino

As fame hit The Jackson Five, the family moved to
Encino, California, which is still their base. The
vast house and large grounds are protected by
electrified gates and guard dogs. Inside, it's
another world. Apart from the many acres for the
family to roam around in, there's a recording
studio, cinema and trophy room.

Family talent
Anyone visiting the Jacksons back in 1970 would
probably have found the brothers out on the
basketball court. There would be eldest brother
Jackie (real name Sigmund Esco), Tito (Toriano
Adaryl), Jermaine (Jermaine LaJaune), Marlon
(Marlon David) and younger brother Randy
(Steven Randall). Although Michael played, he
was never that keen.

And don't forget the Jackson sisters, LaToya
and Janet. In America, they performed with their
brothers on television and in Las Vegas. Today,
they are known for their singing and acting.

By the mid-1970s, Michael's four older
brothers, Jackie, Tito, Jermaine and Marlon, had
followed in their parents' footsteps. All married
young, having children soon afterwards.

Michael still lives at home with his parents,
brother Randy, sisters and pets. Unlike his other
brothers, Michael shyly stays put behind the
electrified gates, avoiding his thousands of fans
who throng the streets of Los Angeles.

The Jackson Five traveled all around the world. This is how the world saw them in the early 1970s. The multi-colored stage costumes *(right* and *far below right)* traveled from America to Africa to Japan. Whether they were relaxing at home *(far top right)* or meeting stars such as Bob Hope *(below)*, the Jackson brothers always remained polite and relaxed, never losing their mischievous sense of humor.

Below: Tito takes his musicianship more seriously than any of the others. Eldest brother Jackie *(right)* usually works out the dance routines for the stage act while Marlon *(below right)*, really knows how to let himself *go.*

Above: Randy, the youngest brother, making his debut playing congas.

Right: Jermaine, a national sex symbol, would prefer being famous for his bass guitar work.

Far left: The Jackson family has such a passion for photography that it's quite common for them to take thousands of photographs while on tour. Here, the photographer just beats Michael to the draw.

Left: Michael at home by the swimming pool, one of the family's favorite places for taking pictures.

Below: Michael with two of his friends who patrol the grounds of "fortress" Encino.

Far left: Michael, the lead singer, taking full control of the audience during a show. When the concert was over, it was quite normal to find him backstage or in his hotel room writing new songs. And when on tour *(left)* he could always try and work out what the foreign magazines have been saying about him.

Below: "Your turn", as Michael lets the audience take over another hit song.

Chapter 3
Growing pains

In 1976, you couldn't miss the headlines in the newspapers: "The Jackson Five are gone. Long live The Jacksons".

Behind the headlines was a story about growing up. At first, The Jackson Five were everybody's favorite, cute little boys. By 1974, they were making some pretty funky records such as *Dancing Machine*. By 1976, they wanted more direct involvement in their own career.

Although they were rich and famous, the Jacksons now had a struggle on their hands. Rock and roll groups usually write their own songs, yet the Jackson family had to *fight* in order to write theirs. In the mid-70s they had an uphill journey.

Fighting to write

In order to have more creative freedom, the family changed record companies. Since Jermaine didn't agree with the move and stayed behind, they changed the group's name. The new outfit was called The Jacksons, consisting of Jackie, Tito, Marlon, Michael and the newest full-time member, Randy.

In 1976 The Jacksons had their own American television show. And in 1977 they performed at the Royal Command Performance in Glasgow.

Destiny

In 1978 they were finally able to write their own songs and had great success with their *Destiny* album. "This is the way we hear music", Michael proudly told anyone who would listen. In 1982, their double *Live* album showed just how much their musicianship and stage style had matured.

In the same year Jermaine rejoined the group. They released a brand new studio album and were set to make a worldwide tour. Take a good look at one of the best-loved music families in the history of pop music: Jackie, Tito, Jermaine, Marlon, Randy and Michael – The Jacksons!

Previous pages: The Jacksons adopted a real live peacock as their mascot because, like their music, it "has all the colors of the rainbow". Notice the peacock lighting arrangement *(right)* on stage, though it's Michael's blazing stage presence that keeps the audience spellbound.

Above and centre: From boy to man. Look at the difference between the chirpy boy of The Jackson Five and the sophisticated moves of Michael today *(opposite)*.

Far left and above: No longer capable of surprising his audiences with speed alone, the mature Michael Jackson makes his dance steps sharper, slicker and altogether breathtaking. Even Hollywood's great Fred Astaire is a fan.

Previous pages: The stage – Michael's second home. Under hot lights, dressed in sparkling clothes, he is renowned for suddenly going from a heart-breaking ballad to a heart-stopping routine. Note two of his most famous trademarks – the white socks under the tuxedo and the glittering glove on his left hand.

Three ways to reduce an audience to tears. When the stage lights are lowered and the spotlight focuses on Michael, it's time for one of those sad, sorrowful songs.

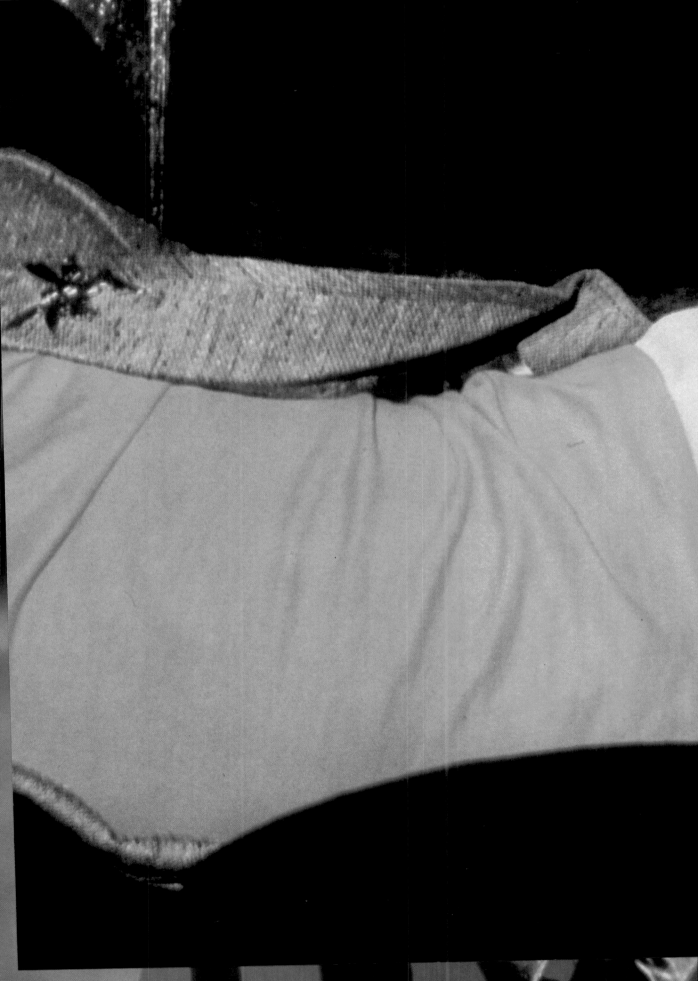

Left: Happy New Year! This was one of the first pictures of Michael taken in January 1983.

Below: By the time this photograph was taken in February, the *Thriller* album had earned itself a "double platinum" award for millions of copies sold.

Previous pages: Michael enjoying a rare moment by himself in Los Angeles, though he certainly wouldn't like it to go on for too long. On more than one occasion he has said "If I lived alone I'd die of loneliness".

Insets: Onstage, Michael demonstrates more of the distinctive style that makes him the most imitated man in contemporary music.

Billie Jean (1983): Michael during the shooting of his great video success (*right* and *far right*). While no one can light up a pavement as Michael does in his film, the fad for red bow ties is still going strong!

Beat It (1983): For the making of this video hit Michael teamed up with 100 members of real life street gangs and heavy guitarist Eddie Van Halen.

Thriller (1983): It's difficult to believe that in real life Michael Jackson is so frightened of horror films that he hates watching them. But he certainly doesn't mind starring in one. Michael had a million-dollar budget to make this 14-minute film.

Previous pages: Michael Jackson turns into a monster in another scene from *Thriller.*

Chapter 5
Into the 90s

"Michael Jackson will be the biggest star of the 1980s and the 1990s". So spoke Quincy Jones a while back. Today, no one doubts him. In 1984, Michael Jackson broke all records by winning eight "Grammy" awards for his *Thriller* album, and his proposed world tour will be the most exciting concert event in years.

Star friends
Just as the great world is moving in on him, Michael is taking a back seat for a while. He stays close to home, letting the world come to him. He freely admits he feels uncomfortable with ordinary "everyday" people.

His closest friends are his pets – a boa constrictor, a llama, two deer, a fawn and several exotic birds. Other friends include the stars Katharine Hepburn, Diana Ross, Jane Fonda, Brooke Shields and Paul and Linda McCartney.

What next?
The future is bright. Michael now has the talent and the finances necessary to turn his hand to any type of project he likes. He loves children, so it's not surprising that one of his side projects was an album about *E.T.* If everyone who works with Michael always seems to have a good word for him, maybe that's because Michael has always been one to give credit to the people who have helped turn his dreams into reality.

Michael Jackson loves the spotlight. He likes being number one. He wears a glittering white glove so he can always feel he's on stage. When he wears that glove, Michael is magic.

It's a night of triumph. Michael Jackson and good friend Brooke Shields at the Motown Records 25th Anniversary party.

Far left: It looks like Michael. There's the red leather jacket, the sunglasses and the white glove. Or is it?

Left: The stars of '83. Michael basking in the success of his video hit *Thriller*, seen here with Jane Fonda, who was almost as successful with her *Workout* album.

Below: Brooke Shields, the American model and actress, hasn't yet made a best-selling record. But she's obviously made a hit with Michael.

Following pages: All that glitters really *is* gold. Here's Michael picking up several awards, along with his good friends Diana Ross and record producer Quincy Jones.

Final Pages: The Jacksons uniting in 1984 for a world tour. They may have been performing now for over twenty years, but the magic they create onstage is still as powerful as ever. From left to right are Tito, Marlon, Jackie, Michael, Randy and Jermaine with his guitar.

THE MICHAEL JACKSON FILE

Full name: Michael Joseph Jackson.
Date of birth: 29 August, 1958.
Height: 5'9".
Color of eyes: dark brown.
First home: 825 Jackson St., Gary, Indiana, USA.
Present home: Encino, California.
First public performance: singing *Climb Every Mountain* in kindergarten.
First record bought: Mickey's Monkey by the Miracles.
First award: in 1965 won talent show at Roosevelt High School, Gary.
First single released: I'm A Big Boy Now on Steeltown Records (unavailable now).
Early musical influences: James Brown, Jackie Wilson (1950s soul singers).
First T.V. appearance: The Hollywood Palace in October 1969 with The Supremes.
First T.V. special: Goin' Back To Indiana with his brothers (1971).
School: grade/high school in Los Angeles. Private tutorial with Rose Fine when on tour.
Later musical influences: all of the Motown artists, The Beatles, The Carpenters and Bread.
Instruments played: piano.
Favorite food: anything healthy. No meat – he's a vegetarian.
Favorite drink: fruit juices.
Favorite car: Rolls Royce.
Favorite film: E.T.
Hobbies: (beside music) drawing with pencil, pen and ink.
Favorite companions: children and animals.
Hates: having his hair pulled, or trying to fix cars. Leaves that to his brothers.
Cherished memory: (non musical) meeting up with Jane Fonda, Henry Fonda and Katharine Hepburn on the set of *On Golden Pond* in 1981.
Pets no longer kept: rats. He had some once, but they ate their babies.
Loves: dancing non-stop; reading best-sellers and books about philosophy; watching favorite films dozens of times; talking to people he can learn something from; visiting museums and getting absorbed in the paintings and sculpture.
Regrets: has never yet managed to do a good oil painting. Maybe one day when there's more time.
Fantasy home: Buckingham Palace.
Favorite clothes: onstage he wears things that are shiny. Offstage, Michael likes things casual.
Ideal night out: spending the time with a good friend. He likes to sit and talk with the lights down. Michael dislikes crowds.
Ambition: to be the best he can, at whatever he does.

DISCOGRAPHY

Albums

Michael Jackson and The Jackson Five
Diana Ross Presents The Jackson Five 1969
ABC 1970
The Jackson Five Christmas Album 1970
Maybe Tomorrow 1971
Goin' Back To Indiana 1971
The Jackson Five's Greatest Hits 1971
Lookin' Through The Windows 1972
Skywriter 1973
Get It Together 1973
Dancing Machine 1974
Moving Violation 1975
Joyful Jukebox Music 1975
The Jackson Five Anthology 1976
Boogie 1979
Motown Superstar Series Volume 12: The Jackson Five 1980
Michael Jackson And The Jackson Five: great songs and performances that inspired the Motown 25th Anniversary T.V. Special 1983

Michael Jackson and The Jacksons
The Jacksons 1976
Goin' Places 1977
Destiny 1978
Triumph 1978
The Jacksons Live 1981

Michael Jackson
Got To Be There 1972
Ben 1972
Music & Me 1973
Forever, Michael 1975
The Best Of Michael Jackson 1975
Off The Wall 1979
Motown Superstars Series Volume 7: Michael Jackson 1980
One Day In Your Life 1981
E.T. The Extra-Terrestrial Storybook 1982
Thriller 1982

Singles

Michael Jackson and The Jackson Five
I Want You Back 1969
ABC 1970
The Love You Save 1970
I'll Be There 1970
Mama's Pearl 1971
Never Can Say Goodbye 1971
Maybe Tomorrow 1971
Sugar Daddy 1971
Little Bitty Pretty One 1972
Lookin' Through The Windows 1972
Corner of the Sky 1972
Hallelujah Day 1973
Get It Together 1973
Dancing Machine 1974
Whatever You Got, I Want 1974
I Am Love 1975
Forever Came Today 1975

Michael Jackson with The Jacksons
Enjoy Yourself 1976
Show You The Way To Go 1977
Goin' Places 1977
Blame It On The Boogie 1978
Shake Your Body (Down To The Ground) 1979
Lovely One 1980
Heartbreak Hotel 1980
Can You Feel It 1981
Walk Right Now 1981

Michael Jackson
Got To Be There 1971
Rockin' Robin 1971
I Wanna Be Where You Are 1972
Ben 1972
With A Child's Heart 1973
We're Almost There 1975
Just A Little Bit Of You 1975
You Can't Win (Part 1) 1979
Don't Stop 'Til You Get Enough 1979
Rock With You 1979
Off The Wall 1979
She's Out Of My Life 1980
Billie Jean 1983
Beat It 1983
Wanna Be Startin' Somethin' 1983
Human Nature 1983
Thriller 1983

Picture acknowledgements:
Colorific!
London Features International
Photo Features International Ltd
Barry Plummer
Pictorial Press
Rex Features
Frank Spooner Pictures
Transworld Features Syndicate

Multimedia Publications (UK) Limited have
endeavored to observe the legal requirements
with regard to the rights of the suppliers of graphic
and photographic materials.

Multimedia wish to acknowledge the assistance of
Stephen Weitzen in the creation of this book.